The Internet

Interesting ways to become part of the online community!

by

Owen Jones

Copyright

Published by Megan Publishing Services
http://meganthemisconception.com
Copyright Owen Jones 2024 ©

Welcome to "Internet Ideas" - a beginner's manual, your guide to mastering the digital realm with confidence and understanding. In today's interconnected world, the Internet has become an essential tool for communication, learning, and entertainment. As a seasoned expert in all things online, I am thrilled to be your guide on this enlightening journey.

This manual has been meticulously curated to provide beginners with a solid foundation for traversing the vast landscape of the Internet. Whether you're connecting for the first time or seeking to deepen your knowledge, this guide will empower you to navigate with ease and make informed decisions. Rest assured that every piece of information presented here is rooted in accuracy and the latest insights.

The Internet, while incredibly powerful, can be complex, but by embarking on this adventure together, you're setting yourself up for success. Equip yourself with the skills and wisdom you need to make the most of the digital age while upholding the values of truth and integrity. Let's begin our exploration of the Internet's boundless possibilities!

I hope that you will find the information helpful, useful and profitable.

The ideas in this ebook on various aspects of the Internet including using it to your advantage is organised into 19 chapters of about 500-600 words each.

I hope that it will interest those who are hoping to make money on line, and those who want to attract more traffic to an offline business by using the often 'free' resources that the Internet has to offer. It will also be useful to bloggers who just want to make friends all over the world and .chat .with them. Luckily, many aspects of the Internet are still free, especially if you don't allow yourself to be manipulated by the self-proclaimed Internet gurus, who are waiting to pounce on unsuspecting newbies.

If you have any feedback, please leave it with the company you bought this book from.

Thanks again for purchasing this ebook.

Regards,

Owen Jones

Owen Jones

Table of Contents

1. Digital Wellness in the Online Era

We all need to trike a balance for our mental and physical well-being in this era where our lives are intricately woven with the digital landscape; finding equilibrium between the online and offline worlds is crucial for maintaining overall well-being. The chapter on "Digital Wellness in the Online Era" delves into the significance of cultivating a healthy relationship with the internet and offers practical insights for navigating the digital realm while prioritising mental and physical health.

The Digital Landscape and its Impact on Well-being

The ubiquity of digital devices has undeniably transformed the way we live, work, and connect. From social media to remote work, the digital landscape has become an integral part of our daily existence. However, the constant connectivity and screen time can take a toll on our mental and physical health.

Excessive screen time is associated with digital eye strain, disrupted sleep patterns, and increased stress levels. Moreover, the addictive nature of social media and the continuous influx of information contribute to what experts term as "digital fatigue." Recognising these challenges is the first step toward achieving digital wellness.

Practical Tips for Managing Screen Time

Balancing the benefits of the digital age with the need for moderation is key to digital wellness. Here are some practical tips for effectively managing screen time:

Set Boundaries: Establish clear boundaries for screen time, both personally and professionally. Designate specific hours for work-related activities and leisure, and stick to these boundaries as much as possible.

Implement the 20-20-20 Rule: To alleviate digital eye strain, follow the 20-20-20 rule. Every 20 minutes, take a 20-second break and look at something 20 feet away. This simple practice helps reduce eye fatigue and maintains visual comfort.

Digital Detox Days: Consider incorporating regular digital detox days into your routine. Choose a day or weekend to disconnect from electronic devices, allowing yourself to engage in activities that promote relaxation and physical activity.

Device-Free Bedrooms: Create a conducive sleep environment by keeping electronic devices out of the bedroom. The blue light emitted from screens can interfere with the production of melatonin, disrupting sleep patterns.

Combatting Digital Fatigue with Mindful Practices

Digital fatigue, often characterised by feelings of overwhelm and burnout, can be mitigated with mindful practices. Here are strategies to combat digital fatigue:

Practice Mindfulness: Incorporate mindfulness techniques into your daily routine. Mindful breathing, meditation, or short breaks for deep breathing exercises can help alleviate stress and improve focus.

Curate Your Digital Space: Declutter your digital environment by organising apps, emails, and notifications. Unsubscribe from unnecessary emails and streamline your digital space to reduce cognitive load.

Set Realistic Goals: Establish realistic and achievable goals for your online activities. Prioritise tasks and avoid overcommitting to prevent feelings of overwhelm.

Fostering a Positive Online Experience

Creating a positive online experience involves cultivating a healthy digital environment and nurturing meaningful connections. Consider the following tips:

Mindful Social Media Use: Be intentional about your social media engagement. Limit time spent on platforms, curate your feeds to include positive content, and unfollow accounts that contribute to negativity.

Digital Hobbies: Explore digital activities that bring joy and fulfilment. Whether it's online courses, digital art, or virtual communities centred around shared interests, engaging in positive online hobbies can enhance your overall well-being.

Establish Digital-Free Zones: Designate specific areas or times in your home where digital devices are not allowed. This helps create spaces for face-to-face interactions, fostering genuine connections with family and friends.

Achieving digital wellness in the online era is about striking a balance that aligns with individual needs and priorities. By implementing practical tips for managing screen time, combatting digital fatigue, and fostering a positive online experience, individuals can navigate the digital landscape while prioritising their mental and physical well-being. In this chapter, readers will discover that the digital era can be a source of enrichment rather than depletion when approached mindfully.

Internet Ideas

2. Blogging as an Art Form

If writing is an art form, then blogging can be seen as an art form too. Blogging is no less an art form than ordinary writing only because it is more popularist and does not require paper. Bloggers write on all sorts of things, in fact they compose pieces on every topic under the sun. People write about their daily lives, their jobs, their hobbies and their problems.

Blogging began life in the mid Nineties for webmasters to maintain a record of their involvement with their computers, which is where the term comes from: 'web log'. Web log became weblogs and then it was contracted to blog. Web logs soon became a well-liked manner of recording and publishing other daily activities on line, much like a diary.

Blogs can get posted to a URL like a website is, or they can be posted to a free bloggers' web site. There are lots of these free blogs, but one of the most famous ones is Google's 'Blogger'.

Despite being free of charge, Blogger offers a fully adaptable blog which can hold adverts like Google Ads and Amazon, so that the blogger can offer related items for sale and make a little money at the same time.

If personal blogs are used to talk about daily life, business blogs can be used as rolling adverts for a company's products. The manager of the firm's blog can compose pieces on innovations, new products, jobs vacant and extraordinary offers. The company's blog can be used as a private press release machine which can reach a global audience.

If you want to create a blog for personal or company use, you will need to know something about blogging, so here are a couple of pointers.

This first thing to do is define what your blog is going to be on. If it is a company blog then that is easy, but a personal blog should have a target audience. It should appeal to a niche group. Try to keep the niche group quite tight, blogs that waffle on colossal sprawling subjects are not as well-liked.

For instance, stamp collecting is far too wide a topic. Collecting British stamps is better, but British commemorative stamps of the 20th Century is even better. Include some images to keep the blog looking cheerful and colourful. This is easily done since most contemporary printers have a facility to scan images and send them to your computer.

In the blogosphere, information is the name of the game. Most people surf to gain information. They surf to get the solutions to worries that they are undergoing; in order to help with their hobbies or only for general information. Therefore, you ought to make your blog a bearer of practical information.

You can make your blog interactive by allowing your readers to leave observations. Some software allows fairly lengthy comments so that visitors can leave their opinions in full. This interactivity will encourage readers to come back to follow the discussion.

In fact, most blogging software will actually inform the leaver of a comment that there has been a reply and it will also harvest the commentator's email address so that you can add them to a mailing list as

long as you provide them with the ability to opt out
of the list if they want to.

3. Using PLR to Kick-start Your Blog

Having a blog can be either a gratifying or a disappointing experience. Gratifying if it is even moderately successful, and a disappointment if no-one ever reads it. A gratifying blog can also lead to a profitable blogging career, and that would make it even more of a pleasure to put one's time into. This article is about one avenue of achieving a level of success as a blogger, that is by using PLR to kick-start your blog.

PLR stands for 'Private Label Rights', which means that you may use the articles as if they were your own with the writer's permission.

First of all, it should be pointed out that hopeful entrepreneurs and communicators are probably starting millions of websites and blogs every month, so your first job is to get above that 'noise level'. In other words, to get your business noticed.

Having a riveting subject for your blog is useful, but not essential. So, what else can you do?

Well, you need to get into the search engines, and there is nothing that they love more than fresh relevant content. It is helpful to see search engines as hungry stray dogs. If you put food out for strays, they will come back for more. If you make a habit of it, they will camp outside your house.

And so will search engines.

When I am not writing novels, I try to create niche content articles (such as this) every couple of days and post them to my site. In January 2021, Google was visiting my blog (http://meganthemisconception.com) every fifteen seconds!

Now, writing meaningful articles might be beyond the ability of newcomers to the job, or to bloggers whose mother language is not English, so my suggested solution to this is to buy targeted content or niche articles and publish them as your own.

Articles that were designed to be used as such are called PLR (Private Label Rights) content. They are written to be resold and reused. The fewer times an article has already been used is an indication of its freshness.

However, no matter how fresh a PLR article is, its user should read it through and change words and phrases to match his or her own style, which will make it your copyright. This will ensure that, if lazier bloggers buy the same blog package later and do not alter it, you will still have an original, personal article.

If you can publish quality new articles perfect for blog posts every other day for two weeks, you will find the search engines waiting at your door.

Internet Ideas

4. Adware

Adware, spyware and anti-virus software share some similarities, one of which is that all three are major problems for computer users. Let's make a distinction between the three.

Spyware is software that does not necessarily harm your computer. What it does is create pathways whereby someone else apart from the computer owner can communicate from that computer. Usually spyware records the different kinds of web sites you go to and sends that information to web advertisers, who then later send you unwanted emails and pop-ups.

Which is why spyware is unpopular and shunned. It is more intrusive than adware. Spyware has its own separate executable programs, which allow it to record your keystrokes, scan files on your hard disks and look at other applications that you use, including but not limited to chat programs, cookies and Web browser settings.

Spyware then sends the data that it had gathered to the spyware author. The author will then use this information for advertising and marketing purposes. They also sell the information to advertisers and other parties.

Adware, on the other hand, is a more legitimate form of software.. It is similar to spyware but adware is advertising spyware which is bundled into free software or a free program and is installed automatically once that particular program or software is loaded into your computer system.

Some kinds of adware, on the other hand, download advertising content when a particular application is being run. Some adware behaves like spyware in that it tracks and reports user data to the program's writers.

The signs of spyware infection include pop-up ads that seem to be irrelevant to the site you are viewing. Sometimes spyware pop-ups are advertisements about adult contents. Furthermore, if you become aware of your computer slowing down, there is a big chance that spyware and its components have found their way into your operating system. If Windows desktop takes a long time to load, it is best to scan your computer for spyware infections.

Viruses, on the other hand, are a harmful form of software. They were designed and created for one reason alone and that is to cause mayhem on your computer. They may destroy whatever data they come in contact with, can initiate self replication and then infect as many components of the computer's operating system or network as possible.

Nowadays, a lot of anti-virus software also provides spyware and adware scanning and removal utilities. They then remove it as well as its components located in the system registry and other places on your computer. It is therefore, good practice to frequently update your anti-virus and anti-spyware scanner to ensure that your computer is protected from the thousands of spyware and viruses in the Internet. Beware of free add-ons or free anything really.

Adware might be spyware in disguise and could be just waiting to be deployed for its writers to gather your information. Learn how to set up a firewall and pop-up blocker in order to minimise the risk of computer infection and ensure the security of all your computer records.

5. Search Engine Optimisation

Internet Marketing and Search Engine Optimisation

Are you thinking about taking the plunge into trying to make some money online? Or perhaps you just want to use the fantastic marketing opportunities that the Internet has to offer to promote an off-line business? It can make the difference between success and mediocrity, but it is certainly not as easy or straight-forward as many people would have you believe. The bottom line is quality. Your online presence has to offer your visitors value for money, and here I mean time as well as expenditure.

Your visitors will want to feel that they have been rewarded for spending time online with you, although this doesn't have to mean money. Information is also important, and unique information is invaluable.

The cheapest way of attracting visitors is SEO or Search Engine Optimisation. In fact, it is an essential way for you to achieve and drive targeted traffic to your site. The quality of the content on your site is what will keep them (returning) there.

SEO is quite complicated, but if you are confident, and you don't mind doing a lot of research, you can do it all yourself. The 'gurus' will want you to buy their services, or their book of tricks, an app, or a subscription to their blog of tips. I suggest that you use all the free trials you can absorb, and read all the free pamphlets on DIY Internet marketing and SEO that you can get your hands on. You will see remarkable increases in the number of visitors to your site. After a few months, you will know your weaknesses, and then you may consider buying specific help, but don't pay a penny until you know what it is that you don't know.

If you see what I mean.

An important part of SEO is using the right keywords so that search engines can properly classify your website, which will make it easier for people who want your stuff to find you online. There is tons of information on this online. Google, the owner of the most important search engine on the planet, is a good source of free information. Getting your keywords and long-tailed keywords right will get you a long way towards your goal. Look out for advice against keyword stuffing, which is using so any keywords in a piece of text that Google will mark your site down, and people will stop visiting because your text sounds unnatural.

The gurus will often try to make you believe that SEO is a dark art that mere mortals cannot hope to understand let alone get right. This is not true, but it is not easy.

The trick is offering quality content and value for money to your visitors. That naturally presupposes that you have visitors. In the beginning, you will be pleased to get five-to-ten a day. Therefore, you can make the content good, and then improve your SEO, or visa-versa.. If you go for the former, you will keep your hard-earned visitors, and they might even recommend your site. On the other hand, if you choose the latter method, your fifty-a hundred visitors might become disappointed with your site, leave and never return.

'You pays your money and takes your choice...' – as the saying goes, but it is not beyond you. Just stick with it.

6. Common Computer Viruses

New computer viruses are being generated, exposed and disabled every day. These computer viruses are developed often just to annoy us and to wreak chaos in our computer systems. Below, I have described ten viruses recently cited as being the most prevalent and being potentially able to inflict the most harm.

However, new viruses are being created on a daily basis, so this list is by no means complete. The best thing you can do is remain vigilant, maintain your anti-virus software updated, and stay aware of the current computer virus threats.

Virus: Trojan.Lodear:
A Trojan (from Trojan Horse) that attempts to download files from a distant source. It will introduce a .dll file into the EXPLORER.EXE process causing system instability.

<u>Virus: W32.Beagle.CO@mm:</u>
A mass-mailing worm that lowers security settings.
It can delete security-related registry sub keys and
may block access to security-related websites.

<u>Virus: Backdoor.Zagaban:</u>
A Trojan that permits the infected computer to be
used as a covert proxy and which may decrease
network performance.

<u>Virus: W32/Netsky-P:</u>
A mass-mailing worm which spreads by emailing
itself to addresses harvested from files on the local
drives.

<u>Virus: W32/Mytob-GH:</u>
A mass-mailing worm and IRC backdoor Trojan for
the Windows platform. Messages sent by this worm
will have the subject chosen randomly from a list
including titles such as: Notice of account
limitation, Email Account Suspension, Security
measures, Members Support, Important
Notification.

<u>Virus: W32/Mytob-EX:</u>
A mass-mailing worm and IRC backdoor Trojan
similar in nature to W32-Mytob-GH. W32.Mytob-

EX runs continuously in the background, providing a backdoor server which allows a distant intruder to gain admittance and control over your computer via IRC channels. This virus spreads by sending itself to email attachments gleaned from your email address book.

Virus: W32/Mytob-AS, Mytob-BE, Mytob-C, and Mytob-ER:

This family of worm variations possesses similar characteristics in terms of what they are able to do. They are mass-mailing worms with backdoor functionality that can be manipulated through the Internet Relay Chat (IRC) network. Additionally, they can spread themselves through email and via various operating system weaknesses such as the LSASS (MS04-011).

Virus: Zafi-D:

A mass-mailing worm and a peer-to-peer worm which replicates itself to the Windows system folder with the filename Norton Update.exe. It can then create a number of files in the Windows system folder with filenames consisting of 8 random characters and a DLL extension. W32.Zafi-D replicates itself to folders with names containing words like 'share', 'upload', or 'music' as 'ICQ 2022 a new!.exe' or 'winamp 5.7 new!.exe'. W32.Zafi-D will also show a fake error message box with the caption "CRC: 04F6Bh" and the text "Error in packed file!".

Virus: W32/Netsky-D:
A mass-mailing worm with IRC backdoor functionality which can also infect computers vulnerable to the LSASS (MS04-011) exploit.

<u>Virus: W32/Zafi-B</u>:
A peer-to-peer (P2P) and email worm that will copy itself to the Windows system folder as a randomly named EXE file. This worm will check for the presence of an Internet connection by attempting to connect to google.com or microsoft.com. A bilingual, worm with an attached Hungarian political text message box which translates to "We demand that the government accommodates the homeless, tightens up the penal code and VOTES FOR THE DEATH PENALTY to cut down the increasing crime. Jun. 2004, Pcs (SNAF Team)"

7. Ebooks for Children

Every parent wants to get their children reading as soon as they can. This means spending a lot of time on daily reading practice sessions. Often children's early reading books are of the interactive type. First readers often have pop-up images to exemplify the key words on the pages.

Why not take this a step further by showing your children multimedia ebooks? Multimedia ebooks for children can take pop-up paper readers to the next degree and more. Even older children may benefit from multimedia ebooks. Educational ebooks on Beethoven, for instance could play snippets from his music.

Ebooks on birds could replay their songs and even short films of birds building their nests or in courtship. There are fantastic opportunities for inventive authors of children's multimedia electronic books.

The ebook could have various modes such as with or without auto-read. The book could read itself out loud and each word could change colour or be underlined as it was being read. The voice could then instruct the child to click on a word to make an event occur, say, replay a bird song or show a short film.

It is frequently hard to hold a child's interest and an interactive ebook like this could be just the means to keep it interesting. This kind of ebook is itself still in its infancy, but it seems that authors of children's books will have to start publishing this way more and more.

One potential problem is children and electronic gadgets. Children nowadays are definitely more used to handling electronic gadgets than any previous generation, but still the hand held ebook readers would have to be very robust and battery operated.

Today's ebook readers normally have screens which are only capable of showing text in black on a white, blue or gray screen, so the displays would have to be capable of full colour and the sound replaying facilities might have to be enhanced. Neither of these enhancements are big problems.

A further advantage of an ebook reader is its ability to modify the size of the text. Children occasionally have problems with their sight and an ebook reader might be just the answer.

It has also been said that some types of dyslexia may be improved if the text is displayed in, say, yellow on a brown background or pink on a blue screen. All combinations are feasible with an ebook reader with a colour screen, such as a notebook.

Home schooling is increasingly popular and school books are being offered to parents at quite a discount to paper books. Paper school books are already costly, but they are bound to rise in price as the world's populace increases and the number of trees for use in paper mills declines.

Ebook readers are fantastic for taking on holiday, if you enjoy reading, because they will hold 3,500 ebooks. This will save you lugging three or four paperbacks on holiday with you next time. It will not be long before each household has a couple of ebook readers.

Internet Ideas

8. *A Guide to the Internet*

There is such a colossal range of choice when it comes to the Net that it can be quite bewildering. The purpose of this article is to make the process of setting yourself up online simpler.

I have been on the Internet since 1988 (with a 2Kb modem in those days) and have used dial-up telephone line connections, high-speed broadband and satellite links.

At whatever point you are thinking about entering the Internet market, you will need an Internet Service Provider (ISP). You may merely want to surf the Internet and exchange emails or you might want your own website as well. Let us talk about these in turn.

The most common kind of UK internet access at the moment is high-speed broadband, whether it comes from a cable provider or a telephone line, usually offered by BY. If you are still using a dial-up 56 Kb connection, you have a magnificent experience in store for you.

If you are thinking about going online for the first time, don't give dial-up a second thought - it is painfully slow, once you have used high-speed broadband.

If you have a cable TV provider, you will almost certainly find it easier to get your connection from your present supplier, otherwise I suggest going with BT Broadband.

BT has lots of experience, a long-standing good record and are very competitive as well nowadays. You can read an piece on broadband Net access by clicking through to BT's web site.

Most ISP's will permit you a couple of email addresses and a limited amount of their disk space to host a personal website. This may be adequate for most individuals, but these days, with lower prices and higher individuality desired, I think that most people would prefer a more personal website and the personal email addresses that go with it.

For example: would you prefer to 'be referred to as'
(ie have an email address of):
Owen1954-8@ntlworld.com and a site address of
http://ntlworld.com/owen1954-8/index.html
or
owen@amiabledragon.com and an address of
http://amiabledragon.com ?

(These are real examples: I was with NTL before, but
have left them and the Amiable Dragon is one of my
websites).
In this instance, amiabledragon.com is my domain
name, so I can put anything I like before it to create
an email address.

It is far more personal AND it can be used for
business, if I like, whereas many ISP's ban the use of
their websites for business purposes. If you opt for
having your own URL, then you will have to host it
somewhere (ie someone will have to store it on their
computer for you).

Finally, you might like to enhance your Internet
experience by upgrading some of your accessories;
for example: buying an optical or radio mouse, a
wireless router, a better chair or desk et cetera.

Internet Ideas

9. Computer Viruses

Everyone who has been on line for more than a few weeks has heard of computer viruses. loads of surfers have had them and loads of surfers have them and do not know it. Not all computer viruses are intended to do damage to the infected computer. Some viruses are meant to steal valuable information such as account numbers and passwords and other viruses are intended to record where you go and what you are interested in.

This information, once gathered, is sent back to the virus' master who will use it to either steal from you or spam you to death with deals based on the words that you have entered into your keyboard. These viruses are also known as tracking cookies. There are also Trojans (Trojan horse), worms and bombs.

There are firms that provide)free of charge) or sell anti-virus software which is designed to protect your computer from these computer viruses. However, because up to several dozen of these viruses are released on a daily basis, you have to have the virus database of your anti-virus software up-dated on a daily basis too. The anti-virus (AV) software virus database is full of all the virus patterns available so far.

It has been estimated that 80% of viruses are intended to destroy data on the computers they infect. That is, they will destroy the file allocation table of your main disk drive making it unreadable, but different viruses do different jobs. I had a virus in December that cleared out my Outlook address book. Two weeks later as I was refilling the address book, and it cleared it out again.

There are a few jobs you can do to minimise your danger of picking up computer viruses. The first thing you have to do is install an AV programme and adjust its settings. Some of the free AV software is as powerful as some of the bought AV software, but if you would like the best, you will have to buy it. It is not expensive - less than $50 a year - especially when you compare it with the price of repairing a damaged computer.

Once you have chosen and installed your AV software, check the options and instruct it to check all incoming and out-going files - that is downloads, uploads and emails. If it will not check emails, it is no use, get another one. Then instruct it to update the pattern files (database) automatically or daily.

Update your patterns and then perform a complete system scan - it can take hours. Then, set the AV software to scan your computer once a week at some time while it will be on, but not in use. I do mine at 2 AM on Monday.

Become wary. Be as suspicious of downloading as you are of strangers prowling about at dusk. Never download from porn sites. Become suspicious of small files. Most viruses, like their living counterparts are tiny. Therefore if you want to download a film or some music and it is much shorter that usual, be cautious or do not do it. Become suspicious of attachments to emails from senders you do not know.

Get anti-spyware software and run it on a regular basis or / and set your browser to dump all cookies at the end of a session (clearing out privacy). If you regularly run into difficulties after dumping the cookies of a site you go to often (like Google), then add them to your 'Trusted Zone'. Computer viruses are out there and can have costly consequences, but you do not have to have them, if you take a few (free) precautions.

10. Article Marketing Tips

Many people who create their first web site get a rude surprise after launching it. They spend a long time thinking about making a website, a long time studying how to build one and a long time making it. They upload it and wait for visitors to flock to it. And nothing happens. No-one comes by. After a while, they might get four or five visitors and then no-one again.

A lot of individuals think that all you have to do is build a web site and it will be registered by the search engines and then people will find it. This is just not true, although you may get indexed after a while. The problem with this tactic is that when people search on a term and the results appear, there are usually several hundred thousand websites. As an unknown site, yours will be close to the bottom of the pile and most people only look at the first page or two of results.

So, the secret is to get your web site listed on the front page of Google's search returns. Article marketing will help your web site rise in the rankings and become visible to your prospective patrons. It is far better to advertise your website so that it will be seen, than to have a flashy website that no-one will ever know about. You can add the bells and whistles later, if you still think it is worth while.

The explanation why writing articles works so well at raising your website's visibility, is because of the way that Google operates. Google attempts to rank websites on their popularity, which is supposed to give an indication of its merit. It gauges popularity by the number of websites that link back to it. These are known as backlinks.

If Google finds a backlink to your website, it checks your website for a mutual backlink to the website that holds one to you. Reciprocal backlinks are not as valuable as non-reciprocal backlinks. When you write an article, you are allowed to put two links back to your website (put one to your home page and one to another page).

If you submit that article to an article distribution

site (and there are hundreds), other web masters may publish your article with its backlinks. The better the article, the more times it will be published, the more solo backlinks you will get and the higher you will climb in Google. The majority of money made on any search term will be made by the websites at the top of the first page.

There are some other ways of obtaining backlinks, but article marketing is by far the best, steadiest long term strategy for promoting a web site.

Who is likely to publish your article? Well, the distribution website for a start, but also newsletter writers, website owners, bloggers and others who require fresh content for their own businesses, but who might not have the time or know-how to write their own articles.

Send your article to article directories and websites like MySpace, where they can be found, read and followed back to your website. Perceive the article as a funnel to your website.

Sign up to blogs or create your own and post them there, but only post relevant articles on other people's blogs.

When you have a quantity of interrelated articles, collate them into a book and give it away or sell it with your backlinks in situ

Put a link on your website to an autoresponder which will deliver your articles to people who sign up for it.

11. Effective Ways to Start Blogging

Everybody has something to say and most people are passionate about something that they would like to talk on. Some people would like to take this desire to talk a couple of stages further - they would like to tell the world about it. That was impossible less that twenty years ago, unless you managed to be on TV or were syndicated in the world's press. Now, of course, anyone can do it.

The Internet makes it possible for everyone to have their say. The young and the old, the rich and the poor can talk about what they like on the Net. You can use a website as your soap box or you could use a specialised web site known as a blog. If you cannot have your own web site for any reason, you could open a free blog at one of the numerous web sites that offer free blogs.

The word 'blog' is short for 'web log' and adding an

piece to your blog is called blogging. Blogs have become a very effective means of spreading one's point of view. The latest kind of blogging is micro-blogging, which is the generic description for Twitter.

Blogging has been used successfully by peoples of countries where the provision of human rights is not a government priority. Just recently, dissidents in Iran, Iraq and Myanmar have kept the world up-to-date on repression in their countries through blogs. The blogs were often reprinted in the world press and reported on the International news.

If you want to blog for free, search Google for 'free blogs' and take a look about. There are dozens of free blog sites about and they all offer different features. Blogger by Google is one of the better ones, but there really are many different types of free blogs.

One consideration is whether you want your blog to be open or closed. That is, do you want anyone to be able to read it or do you want just a closed user group (CUG), which could be your friends, your family or your colleagues.

It should not take longer that thirty minutes to set

up your blog. Some providers like to approve new blogs, but others do not. You could be blogging within the hour, so write an article welcoming people to your blog and post it to the blog. Make it 'sticky' if you can, so that it is always the first post that visitors read when they arrive at your blog.

Make your posts educational and attempt to keep them newsworthy. They ought to neither be so short that it is not worth coming to read them nor so long that they get boring – 400 to 500 is believed to be about right.

You will have to promote your blog or no-one will know that it is there. Do this by posting your pieces (with your blog address affixed) to a couple of article directories. It is free and will give your blog a real boost in circulation. You can give up doing this when your blog is self-sustaining.

Permit all visitors to make comments on the blog, because it encourages people to come back, but check frequently for spam comments and delete them because a blog full of spam looks neglected.

Internet Ideas

12. Internet Business Opportunities

There are obvious advantages of having an Internet business over having a traditional business in a store on the high street. However, a traditional high street shop also has benefits. For instance, you have to be there every day or the store is not open and people will walk past your store. The disadvantages are that you will have to stock the store and pay rent.

An Internet business is less expensive to set up; you might not need stock and it can run and make money for a couple of days without you or anyone else being there. If you set up your Internet business correctly. As with all efficient jobs, a lot of the work goes on behind the scenes. Internet business opportunities are not different.

The benefits of Internet business opportunities over high street businesses are that possible earnings are limited only by the number of people online, not the number of people who walk down your street; start up costs are very low, although time spent establishing the business can be higher and you do not have to be present to make a sale, so you can sell twenty-four hours a day, seven days a week.

Internet sales are mushrooming. In fact, the Baby Boomers were disinclined to give their credit card details over the Internet until banks promised immunity from Internet fraud. The children of the Baby Boomers have no such reluctance and neither do their children. Not only that, but as more and more formerly 'poor' countries become developed, they too are using the Internet to shop on line.

When the Chinese and the Indians start shopping on line there will be a global boost to sales the size of which has never been witnessed in global history. Both India and China have more than a billion inhabitants, many or whom are deprived, but their economies are growing at about ten percent a year. How many of those people are going on line every day with a credit card in their pocket?

They also wish for the items that Westerners have or wish for. They have seen them on TV and in the films. They desire new technology and very soon they will be buying it.

Hobbies are a great place to start. Only people who have free time can indulge in hobbies. Poor people, I mean Third World poor people, only work and sleep. When Asia becomes affluent enough to have time for hobbies, make certain that you are ready and now is the time to prepare.

Tourism is another beneficial starting point. Many Asians are already travelling abroad. Mostly in Asia and generally in guided package tours, but the tendency is there. Travel agencies, hotels, tour buses and associated industries should get prepared.

If you are searching for Internet business opportunities the time has never been better. Within the next couple of years confidence will return in the West and credit cards will start coming out in the East. Now is the time to think about a career online and search for a couple of Internet business opportunities.

Internet Ideas

13. How to Generate Sales with a Viral E-book

Are you aware of the idea of viral marketing? Viral advertising is a way of persuading other people to pass your web site's URL or address around the Net for you. It is a similar concept to the old fashioned chain letter, but not quite the same.

The trick is to compose something so interesting to so many people that surfers who read it will send it on to their friends and family. And your contact details are attached at the end of it.

Viral marketing can show your contact details to thousands, hundreds of thousands or even millions of surfers in a very short time and for no financial outlay. It is one of the most efficient types of promotion known to the Internet Marketer.

There are two principal ways of starting the viral

advertising snowball rolling down hill. The fastest way is to find or compose a very funny joke, append your contact details to the bottom of it and send it to your friends and family. They will pass it on and the snowball is off. The only difficulty with this approach is that the message is not targeted.

In other words if you are selling insurance you want to have your contact details in front of people older than the age of 18, but you have no control over who reads your joke. Half of the people reading it might be children who do not have a credit card or require insurance anyway.

If you would like to reach a targeted audience, then you have to put a bit more work into your campaign, but not that much more. This method involves writing an ebook on the advantages of insurance and sending that to your friends and family. They will send it to their friends, if it is interesting enough, but no-one would send it to kids, would they?

Hey presto, thousands of adults who almost certainly have a credit card and require insurance of some sort have your useful information on insurance and your contact details. This approach works for most concepts. Do you have web site on the Net game

'Halo'?

Excellent, write about Halo mods (modifications) and send that out. Very few kids would pass that on to adults, but they may ask their parents to buy them Halo for Christmas. Viral advertising is free and other people do your marketing for you. The 'only' thing that you have to do is compose an ebook (or report) that is interesting enough for people to want to pass on.

There are a couple of of interesting variations to this simple ebook. You could fill it full of associate links to items. If someone buys anything after clicking on one of your links, you will earn a commission. If they join the same scheme from your link, you will earn a payment off all of their sales too.

In the same vein, you could permit surfers passing the book on to join your sales structure (downline) and rebrand the book as if it were theirs. This gives all the Internet Marketers who see it a better reason for sending it on and you still earn a proportion of their sales. You could soon have thousands of people in your downline earning you commission.

Internet Ideas

14. Internet Marketing Secrets

You are reading this, so it is obvious that you already do some stuff on line, but how much do you use the Internet? Do you use it to its full potential? Do you just spend money on the Net or do you create money on the Internet too?

You might say that you have never spent a penny on line, but that would not be true, would it? You have a computer that you almost certainly use mostly for going on line and you pay for a broadband connection.

If you find yourself only surfing to use up free time, why not set yourself the goal of using the Net to pay for your monthly connection fees and your next (replacement) computer or a new laptop? That could be a project, a quest, a challenge, if you like.

If you have a surfeit of time on your hands this

would be a decent excuse to extend your knowledge of computers, the Net and business or business on line as well.

If you already have a business, on or off line, you ought to be using the Internet to advertise it. If you are unfamiliar with the on line ways of marketing, we can stick with traditional off line ways that have been imitated on line.

For example, there are thousands of free on line classified ad web sites. Just enter 'free classified ads' into Google and stand back!

However, classifieds are generally perceived as not being as effectual as their off line counterparts. This is because people spam these free ads web sites from all over the world merely for a free back link and so loads of the ads are irrelevant or not local.

Another kind of on line advertising copied from the 'real world' is banner marketing. Business people can pay to have a banner placed on a relevant website in order to promote their companies. It is equivalent to having a big advertisement in a newspaper.

Unfortunately, this kind of marketing does not work

on line so well as it does off line either. Specialists say that surfers expect things for free on line, so their eyes 'look through' banner adverts.

So how can you promote your business on line? Well, believe it or not, it by using the really top, up-market off line promoting techniques of having recommendations, reviews and pieces written about the goods that you are marketing. This would cost thousands or more in a newspaper, but it is practically free on line.

The number one best way of advertising on line is to write pieces on or about the subject of your products or company and posting them to article directories with your URL in the byline. This will give you a back link which Google values very highly in working out your firm's ranking in their search engine.

Internet Ideas

15. Is It Safe to Download Computer Software from the Internet?

Do you ever wonder whether it is safe to download items off the Internet? I know that I am asked that question several times a month. The fact is, that it depends, like most answers. It depends on two fundamental factors: how good your defences are and where you are downloading from.

You might be thinking: well, if my defences are decent, why would it matter where I download from and that is a good question, but so is: what do you think of as decent protection?

If your idea of good protection is a free version of Avira, then you are going to have trouble. One day or another you will have trouble, guaranteed. I can say that with my hand on my heart, because they have a paid version too. If the free version is as decent as the paid version, why do surfers pay?

Because they are stupid? I do not think so. By the way, I am not having a go at Avira! They give away a marvellous product and as long as you are careful, it may be all you require. Avira and all the other good anti-virus software suites require a little help to keep you secure.

For example, they will require you to run a firewall at the same time and use an anti-spyware program on a frequent basis. They will also need you to not put yourself at the greatest risk either by visiting certain kinds of sites and not opening attachments from people you do not trust.

If you run the free forms of these AV software programs, you will notice that certain features like the firewall or and the email attachment scanner have been disabled. This is how you will pick up viruses. Another way that you lay yourself open to concerns is by downloading free utilities. These pieces of software almost always include tracking routines.

The software will do its job, but it will install a tracking cookie on your computer which will phone home every day to its boss and tell them where you have been surfing, so that they can spam you with like things.

Porn sites are another good instance of dangerous web sites. You get 'free porn', but they get your IP address and possibly your email address too, which means that they are able to either spam you themselves or and sell your email address on so that half the world can spam you.

So, free AV software is OK, but you have to help it. On the other hand paid software from a reputable firm like Norton, Kaspersky and Nod, to name but a few, should take care of you without you having to do anything but pay and install and permit automatic updates. You can expect that from these firms and they can deliver that degree of protection for $50-60 a year and then you can download anything you like.

The Internet is very much a case of 'you pays your money and you takes your choice' and 'free' is certainly not always the best choice.

Internet Ideas

16. Home Schooling and Learning by Computer

There is a computer in virtually each home in the West these days and the rest of the world is catching up very quickly. Therefore, it is extremely important for you to have one at home too, because of the many benefits it can bring, especially if you have an Internet connection.

Nowadays, you have to have some computer knowledge, if you would like even a half-decent job, so learning how to use a computer has to start at school.

You and your child can have a unique educational experience with a computer at home. Children of today ought to learn about this very important device at the very earliest age possible and one of the best ways to do that is through home schooling computer programs.

Internet Ideas

Currently, even pre-school children are being taught how to operate computers and their associated peripherals. If you choose home schooling, you and your child will also spend much of your time using a computer and the Net.

Educating your children can be far better when done online, because of the various resources obtainable there. Your child will be offered with exceptional educational resources, from which he/she will benefit greatly not least since employment market trends today mostly involve the Net.

One of the largest ethnic factions that likes to make use of home schooling is the African Americans because many see some society problems and they can keep themselves informed on their own history by home schooling.

The parents of children from minority classes can help their offspring learn more about their history by using an Internet connection at home.

A child's education can be best encouraged by parents and they can also help in strengthening the mindset of their children as well. Parents container educate their children about their own particular traditions with the various online resources.

It is important to keep in mind that home schooling only works properly, if the parents are prepared to give their children their full support. They must also be committed and prepared for the challenges that they will run into. The parents ought to look for a particularly good computer program or book to help their children learn about utilising computers.

Often, the lessons are divided into several sections or series in order that the children may learn them easily. Children have different learning capacities and since sometimes children are not given much chance in traditional schools, the use of computers is an ideal opportunity for you to bring out the best in them.

Home schooling is no longer out of the ordinary, so if you think that your child is not doing well in school, talk to his tutors and get some details regarding your child. The school guidance counsellor can also assist you to select the best education for you child. Home schooling is already accepted and perhaps it might help your child to learn more in the environs of your own home.

If you are prepared to commit yourself to home schooling, you will need to discuss the subject with your child. You could start by asking your child about his experience in school and then raise the topic of home schooling. See what your child thinks of the idea.

Explain its benefits. You could say that computer learning will be easier. It is better if you and your child both agree on home schooling, since you will have to do it closely together.

There are lots of home schooling programs to select from so it could take a number of weeks before you can find the appropriate one.

17. Internet Scams

If you have been on the Internet long enough to set up some kind of email address, you will probably have been invited to earn some extra money by filling in on line surveys.. These so-called paid on line surveys are aimed at the growing number of people who stay at home all day with a computer, little capital and no work. They are particularly aimed at stay at home mums and the unemployed.

It is possible to earn a few dollars a month from some of these on line survey businesses, but many of them are cons. They can make their money in a variety of ways, but usually the cash out figure for the person surveyed is quite high, often $50 or $100.

It is hard to attain that figure at the rate of one $1 survey per week. However, they have you traipsing back and forth to their website in the hope that you will click on one of their adverts and they will get paid.

The first sign of a scam survey firm is the up front registration fee. This is typically less than $50 and seems a good deal if you are going to be earning the thousands of dollars that they 'promise'. Well, not really promise, because the disclaimer always states that you may not earn as much as the 'people' who have sent in the testimonials that you read plastered all over their web sites.

Testimonials from people like 'Mary T., New York', completely undetectable, unverifiable, probably fabricated 'people', who claim to be earning enough money completing on line surveys to pay off the mortgage, buy a big car and go on holiday in the Seychelles every year. Rule number one for avoiding on line scams: never pay a fee on the assurance of possibly earning money.

The cell phone rip-off is always very popular amongst con men and women. In this scam, you will be asked to authenticate that you are a real person by replying to a straightforward text message. What you are not told though is that you are texting a premium number which will probably cost you up to $5. The company is sure that you will not notice this charge, especially if you are pay-as-you-go and do not receive monthly bills.

Another popular dodge is where you are promised special offers or even cash for clicking on the banners of the site's 'partners'. You will be asked to seek more details by clicking on a banner. You may be promised 30% off or five cents for clicking. What you are not told is that you will be plagued from now to kingdom come by telesales people. Health insurance, pet insurance, free holidays, you name it. The only thing that you can be certain of is that you will end up paying more.

Then there is the free magazine con. You are offered a free magazine on an interesting topic of your choice. Again they ask for your telephone number. What they do not say is that your free magazine comes with a subscription to their magazine which costs $19.95. The payment will be made to your phone bill and you will probably never even notice it, which is what they are hoping for.

Never give out sensitive information over the Internet if you do not know who is receiving it. Phishing is also a profitable swindle, where an email purports to come from a bank or even Google or

Yahoo. You are told that your account has been hacked and that you should confirm your details. As soon as you do, your account will be hacked sure enough.

18. How to Monetise Your Web Site

Making money from e-commerce is not as easy as it used to be because of the huge amount of competition. Therefore, you have to use each trick in the book to create multiple income streams from your web site and you have to give (prospective) customers a reason to go to your web site.

There are numerous types of web sites possible, but I find that specialised niche sites are the simplest to monetise. So, rather than writing on 'gardening', write on 'orchids' and better still would be 'orchids from Thailand' or even 'orchids native to northern Thailand'.

Taking this example, you should know something about the subject or at least have an interest in the topic. If you do not have enough knowledge to write at least five web pages, you need to do some research.

First, design and produce your web site, then write your front or home page. This page can either be a 'welcome to our web site on Thai orchids from northern Thailand' type page or you can merely jump straight in to the subject or you could compose a short welcoming paragraph and the rest of the page giving an introduction to the issue matter of the site.

Then create a couple more web pages and see which way the site is trending, because this can affect the sort of marketing you use. The next thing you need is a couple of suppliers. For this sort something like 'suppliers of Thai orchids affiliate program' into Google and see what comes up. (I just checked Thai orchids and there are Thai suppliers).

Sign up as an affiliate or enquire of them to create you an agent. Most of the suppliers of various things have their own banners and photos (known as 'creatives') for their affiliates to use. Decide on adverts that fit in with the style of your site and place them at suitable points in the actual body text. Have the text wrap around the ad creatives so that they cannot be missed.

Keep these adverts as applicable as possible to the issue matter. Then go to Google Adsense, open an account if you do not have one and follow the directions to make adverts that fit in with the structure of your pages. There is stacks of advice and theory on where to put what on Google's Adsense site.

Scatter two or three of those around your site too. Then go to a more general gardening affiliate web site where they sell accessories and add a couple of adverts on flower pots, hanging baskets, gardening tools and that sort of thing. Also put a few ads about garden furniture.

If you are stuck for ideas on pieces on Thai orchids write a few filler pieces on gardening tools and oak garden furniture too. Then you could look for publications on (Thai) orchids. Go to Amazon, open an account, and pick a couple of books on Thai orchids. Put their creatives on relevant pages and sell books. If you can find a magazine, become an affiliate and sell subscriptions.

And last but not least, have somewhere where people can join your newsletter. This way you construct a specialised list of gardeners who are interested in (Thai) orchids and you can send them not-to-be-missed special offers in your monthly newsletter.

Internet Ideas

19. Podcasting Prowess

In the vast landscape of digital content creation, podcasting has emerged as a powerful and dynamic platform for individuals to share their voices, stories, and expertise. This chapter, titled "Podcasting Prowess" serves as a comprehensive guide for those looking to venture into the captivating world of podcasting. From the essentials of podcast creation to the intricacies of building a loyal audience, let's uncover the art of podcasting.

The Resonance of Podcasting

Podcasting has witnessed an unprecedented surge in popularity, becoming a favoured medium for creators and consumers alike. What sets podcasts apart is the intimate and immersive experience they offer. Unlike other forms of content, podcasts enter the ears of the audience, forging a unique connection through the power of spoken words.

Diving into Podcast Creation

Choosing Your Niche:

The first step in podcasting prowess is defining your niche. Whether it's true crime, personal development, or niche hobbies, selecting a focused and interesting topic lays the foundation for a successful podcast.

Crafting Compelling Content:

Once your niche is established, crafting engaging content is key. Consider creating an outline for your episodes, ensuring a balance between structured segments and spontaneous discussions. High-quality content is the bedrock of any successful podcast.

Investing in Essential Equipment:

While podcasting can be accessible to beginners, investing in some essential equipment can significantly enhance the quality of your production.

A good microphone, headphones, and audio recording software are essential for delivering a professional sound.

Navigating the Digital Soundscape: Equipment Essentials

Microphone Selection:

Selecting the right microphone is crucial for delivering clear and crisp audio. USB microphones like the Blue Yeti or XLR microphones like the Shure SM7B are popular choices among podcasters. Choose one that aligns with your budget and recording environment.

Headphones:

Quality headphones are your auditory window into the world of your podcast. Closed-back headphones, such as the Audio-Technica ATH-M50x, provide excellent sound isolation and ensure a focused recording experience.

Audio Editing Software:

Invest time in learning audio editing software like Audacity, GarageBand, or Adobe Audition. These tools enable you to fine-tune your recordings, add music or effects, and produce a polished final product.

Crafting a Podcasting Strategy: Content Strategies

Consistency is Key:

Establish a consistent release schedule for your episodes. Whether it's weekly, bi-weekly, or monthly, consistency builds anticipation and loyalty among your audience.

Engaging with Your Audience:

Create avenues for audience interaction, such as listener Q&A segments or social media shout-outs. Engaging with your audience fosters a sense of community and strengthens your connection with listeners.

Guest Collaborations:

Consider inviting guests relevant to your podcast's theme. Guest collaborations not only bring fresh perspectives but also expand your podcast's reach as guests share the episode with their networks.

Reaching Audiences through the Power of Spoken Words

Optimising for Discoverability:

Ensure your podcast is discoverable by optimising your episodes for search engines. Craft compelling episode titles and descriptions, and use relevant keywords to improve visibility.

Utilising Social Media:

Leverage social media platforms to promote your podcast. Share behind-the-scenes glimpses, episode teasers, and engage with your audience through comments and direct messages.

Submitting to Directories:

Submit your podcast to popular directories like Apple Podcasts, Spotify, and Google Podcasts. Being listed on these platforms increases your podcast's visibility and accessibility to a wider audience.

The Exciting World of Growing Your Podcast

Growing a podcast involves a mix of strategic planning and organic development. Monitor listener feedback, adapt to changing trends, and continuously refine your content to keep your audience engaged.

Monetisation Strategies:

Explore monetisation avenues such as sponsorships, affiliate marketing, or listener donations. As your podcast gains popularity, these strategies can turn your passion project into a sustainable endeavour.

Analytics and Metrics:

Leverage podcast analytics to understand your audience's preferences. Track metrics like download numbers, listener demographics, and episode popularity to refine your content strategy and identify areas for improvement.

Networking within the Podcasting Community:

Engage with other podcasters, join podcasting forums, and attend industry events. Networking within the podcasting community opens doors to collaboration opportunities, cross-promotion, and valuable insights from experienced creators.

With the right equipment, content strategy, and audience engagement, your podcast can become a resonant voice in the digital soundscape, reaching and connecting with listeners around the world. So, don your headphones, hit record, and let your podcasting journey begin.

Internet Ideas

Owen Jones

Contact Details

Facebook: AngunJones
Twitter: @owen_author
Blog: Megan Publishing Services

This book is part of the 'How to...' series of 125 manuals by Owen Jones.
Links to the whole series in many languages can be found on:
Megan Publishing Services
https://meganthemisconception.com